W9-ATH-758

THE ERIE CANAL

THE ERIE CANAL

Illustrated by Peter Spier

DOUBLEDAY

New York London Toronto Sydney Auckland

Published by Doubleday, a division of Bantam Doubleday Dell Publishing Group, Inc., 666 Fifth Avenue, New York, New York 10103 **Doubleday** and the portrayal of an anchor with a dolphin are trademarks of Doubleday, a division of Bantam Doubleday Dell Publishing Group, Inc. Library of Congress Catalog Card Number 70-102055 ISBN 0-385-05234-0 Illustrations copyright © 1970 by Peter Spier *Low Bridge! Everybody Down (or Fifteen Years on the Erie Canal)* by Thomas S. Allen Copyright 1912 and renewed 1940 Copyright assigned to Jerry Vogel Music Co., Inc., 121 W. 45th Street, New York, N.Y. 10036 Used by permission of copyright owner All Rights Reserved Printed in the United States of America

I've got an old mule and her name is Sal,

Fifteen miles on the Erie Canal.

She's a good old worker and a good old pal,

Fifteen miles on the Erie Canal.

We've hauled some barges in our day,

Filled with lumber, coal, and hay,

And ev'ry inch of the way we know

From Albany to Buffalo.

Low bridge, ev'rybody down!

Low bridge, for now we're going through a town.

You can always tell your neighbor,

You can always tell your pal,

If you ever navigated on the Erie Canal.

We better get along on our way, old gal,

Fifteen miles on the Erie Canal.

You bet your life I'd never part with Sal,

Fifteen miles on the Erie Canal.

Git up there, mule, here comes a lock,

We'll make Rome 'bout six o'clock,

So one more trip and then we'll go

Right straight back to Buffalo.

Low bridge, ev'rybody down!

Low bridge, for now we're going through a town.

You can always tell your neighbor,

You can always tell your pal,

If you ever navigated on the Erie Canal.

On July 4, 1817, the Erie Canal was begun at Rome, New York. Upstate New York was then a wilderness of swamps and forests filled with game. Utica was a frontier post, Syracuse a dismal hamlet. And there were Indians—often unfriendly. In October 1825 "Clinton's Big Ditch" (nicknamed for Governor DeWitt Clinton, 1769-1828) was completed without the aid of a single professional engineer. The chief engineers were actually two New York lawyers. It was one of the engineering marvels of the world: 363 miles long from Albany to Buffalo, cut through the wilderness, 40 feet wide and 4 feet deep, connecting the Great Lakes with the Atlantic Ocean. There were 18 aqueducts which carried the canal across rivers, and there were 83 locks. The rise from the Hudson River to Lake Erie was 568 feet. The cost of the canal had been $7,143,789. To pay for it, tolls were levied on traffic. Now the nation had for the first time a cheap and fast route through the Appalachian Mountains, which until then had been a solid barrier between East and West. Freight, traveling the dirt path between Albany and Buffalo by 8-horse wagon, took from 15 to 45 days, at $100 per ton. Canalboats did it in 9 days for $6 a ton! Between 1835 and 1862 a new Erie Canal was built: wider, deeper, and with double locks for speed. In 1882 tolls, totaling $42 million since the canals had opened, were abolished. In 1917—a hundred years after Clinton's Ditch was begun—the Erie Canal ceased operations when the New York Barge Canal was opened. The Erie Canal had been instrumental in developing the country's interior and in opening up the West.

Thousands of school children annually visit the Canal Museum in Syracuse, New York, located in the building where canalboats were weighed on a mighty cradle scale to determine the toll due. The curator told me that these are the questions asked of him most often: *How fast did the boats go?* A packet, pulled by fresh horses, covered 80 miles in 24 hours, but carried only passengers and hand luggage. Line boats (freight) made 2 miles an hour and took 9 days to travel from Albany to Buffalo. Log rafts—up to 500 feet long—slowly pulled by oxen, held up traffic at locks and were therefore hated by canallers. The speed limit was 4 miles per hour. Boats could travel at night as well as during the day. *What did the boats carry?* Line boats carried countless immigrants, supplies, manufactured goods, guns, and tools westward; then returned with potatoes, flour, apples, whiskey, lumber, and furs. *What did canal children do?* Most captains and their families lived on board and spent virtually all their lives on the canal. Children tended the animals and helped run the boat as soon as they were old enough. They went to school only when the canal was closed by ice from December through March. *Where did canal people go to church?* There were numerous church boats on the canal, and there were churches in the towns that sprang up along the canal. *Where did canal families shop?* General stores were located near most locks and on the "wide-waters," where boats were kept during the winter and where they could turn around. *How much did canal workers earn?* Monthly wages in 1823: captain, $30; steersman, $15; steward, $12; hostler, $10; cabin boy, $4.80. *How much did a canalboat cost?* From $1500 to $5000. *What did travel cost?* Packet rates in 1835: through passengers 5¢ per mile with meals and lodgings. Way passengers 3¢ per mile, dinner 37½¢, supper and breakfast 25¢, lodging 12½¢. *What were the toll rates?* In 1863: bacon per 100 pounds per mile: 1/10 of 1¢. Deer, buffalo, and moose skins per 1000 pounds per mile: 3/10 of 1¢. Passenger boats: 4¢ per mile. *Where were the animals kept?* Each line boat had its own stable forward. Mules went on and off the boat—steered by the tail—over the "horse bridge," which was stored on the roof. The man driving the team was called the "hoggee" and walked behind them on the towpath. *How many animals pulled a boat?* 3 horses pulled 1 packet. Two mules towed 1 line boat, but 3 mules towed 2 boats butted together. The first boat hoisted its rudder out of the way, the second steered. *How did boats pass each other without tangling towlines?* One boat would move to the far side of the canal, its mules halted on the outside of the towpath. The towline—100 feet to 150 feet long—would then sink to the bottom of the canal, and the overtaking or oncoming boat could pass freely. *Why were the bridges so low?* Canal building crews had to construct bridges as they divided farms and cut roads with the canal. A low bridge took less timber than a high one and was much cheaper! *Can you still see the old canal?* All along the old canal route there are remnants of the Erie Canal. Some sections are dry moats, others are full of water, and still other stretches have been filled in. Many of the old locks and aqueducts can still be seen, especially around Montezuma and Port Byron, where lock Number 52 sits right next to the New York State Thruway.

Moderato

I've got an old mule and her name is Sal, Fif-teen miles on the Er-ie Can-al. She's a

good old work-er and a good old pal, — Fif-teen miles on the Er-ie Can-al. — We've

hauled some bar-ges in our day, Filled with lum-ber, coal, and hay, — And ev'ry inch of the

Chorus

way we know From Al-ban-y to Buf-fa-lo. — Low bridge, ev-'ry bod-y down!

Low bridge, for now we're go-ing thru a town. You can al-ways tell your neigh-bor, You can al-ways tell your pal, If you

ev-er nav-i-ga-ted on the Er-ie Can-al. — Er-ie Can-al. —

2. We'd better get along on our way, old gal,
Fifteen miles on the Erie Canal.
You bet your life I'd never part with Sal,
Fifteen miles on the Erie Canal.
Git up there, mule, here comes a lock,
We'll make Rome 'bout six o'clock,
So one more trip and then we'll go
Right straight back to Buffalo.

Low bridge, ev'rybody down!
Low bridge, for now we're going through a town.
You can always tell your neighbor,
You can always tell your pal,
If you ever navigated on the Erie Canal.

ABOUT THE AUTHOR

In 1952 Peter Spier came to New York from Amsterdam, where he was born and educated. Since that time he has established himself as one of this country's most gifted children's book authors and illustrators. Among the many prestigious awards he has won are the Caldecott Medal, the Caldecott Honor Award, the Boston Globe-Horn Book Award, and the American Book Award. His work can be found in museums and private collections across the country. He and his wife, Kay, the parents of two children, live in Shoreham, New York.